Out of Darkness, Light

The John B. Lee
Signature Series

Out of Darkness, Light

April Bulmer

First Edition

The John B. Lee Signature Series

Hidden Brook Press
www.HiddenBrookPress.com
writers@HiddenBrookPress.com

Out of Darkness, Light
by April Bulmer

Editor – John B. Lee
Cover Design – Richard M. Grove
Layout and Design – Richard M. Grove
Front Cover Photograph – "Goddess Healing Energy"
                                    Photo by Healing63 – depositphotos.

Typeset in Garamond
Printed and bound in Canada
Distributed in USA by Ingram, in Canada by Hidden Brook Distribution

Library and Archives Canada Cataloguing in Publication

Bulmer, April, 1963-, author
        Out of darkness, light / April Bulmer.

Poems.
ISBN 978-1-927725-54-2 (softcover)

        I. Title.

PS8553.U49O98 2018   C811'.54   C2018-902732-0

I wish to thank Black Moss Press
and Hamilton Arts & Letters
for their funding through
the Writers' Reserve program
at the Ontario Arts Council.
The Ontario Arts Council
is an agency of
the Government of Ontario.

I would also like to thank
Arts Connect Cambridge
for their 2018 grant.

Thank you to my mother and soulmate Lichee,
Lee Anne Johnston for her ongoing friendship
and literary support and
the Cambridge Writers Collective.

I also wish to thank Trudi and George Down
at the Book Band and Idea Exchange, Preston.

Special thanks to Richard Grove (Tai) at
Hidden Brook Press and John B. Lee.

I am grateful for the family and friends in my life
who support me in a variety of ways.

Contents

Darkness and Light in the poems of April Bulmer

Imagine the fertile womb, the goddess of river and earth, the moonlight and menses of prayer, the dimming of darkness with light, the flowering of candle in flame, the trimmed wick and the softening wax of its burning, the communion of alluvial soil and bursting seed, the flow of healing waters, the slaking of spiritual thirst, the blooming of life and the crossing of shadows and shades of the grave and you have entered the world of Bulmer's lovely metaphysical poetry where the metaphysics are simplified by the clarity of luminous lines. Informed by the story of creation involving the rib of Adam and the apple of Eve, this garden of April Bulmer is fertile and flowering where life is rooted in the womb of woman. The opening poem celebrates the "curve of light/ and heart/ a red fruit./ Girdle of bone." The river of these poems is wide hipped, fecund with turtles and alive with fish. Moonlight floods the water and blood flows with the spirit of life. "Once I loved a boy/ his eyes the shade/ of copper coins." She writes in one poem. "How quiet my heart/ a still pond/ in the dim." She writes in another. She does not shy away from sex, but celebrates its glory in lines from "Honey" where she extolls the beauty of congress "Touch me husband/ and I swell." There's something of the blending of the spiritual and the sensual that these poems share with the Biblical "Song of Solomon." In her preface she introduces the reader to a sisterhood she calls "The Congregation of Women." She tells us that as they gather by the banks of the Grand near Cambridge they pray for love, children, health and spiritual blessing and in doing so thereby battle the forces of darkness with the powers of light. And so in these poems we experience that blessing. We share in the light. In the words of her final poem "...in the morning/ ...the sun/ ... Goddess, her bright reflection:/ her soft, pierced ears." And we experience the consolation of that light. We share in its blessing.

John B. Lee
Poet Laureate of the city of Brantford in perpetuity
Poet Laureate of Norfolk County for life

Preface to *Out of Darkness, Light*

"Ex Tenebris Lux" or "Out of Darkness, Light" was the motto of St. Lucia. Lucia or Lucy means light and bears the same root as "lucid" which suggests clear radiance. St. Lucia (283-304) is patron saint of the blind and those with eye trouble, as well as patron saint of Syracuse, Sicily where she was born.

She became a Christian martyr after she endured abuse at the hands of Romans and survived. The significance of her martyrdom was integrated into an existing Scandinavian festival celebrating the winter solstice and preventing the mischievous activity of witches and evil spirits. Lucy still represents the rebirth of light. In Sweden, Denmark and other Scandinavian countries, as well as Italy and parts of Germany, a young girl is chosen at this time to portray Lucy and to wear a white gown and a crown of burning candles.

Celebrations of light during the darkest time of the year are also Christian and Jewish themes. The birth of Jesus, often regarded as the light of the world, is celebrated in December and so is Hanukkah, the festival of light.

But these poems are written from the perspective of the fictional Congregation of Women in Cambridge, Ontario who worship in a variety of ways, mostly feminist. They invoke many deities and spiritual forces including Christ, the Goddess and St. Lucy, herself. They are led in worship by Mother Scarlett: "her hair long and red as serpents."

The Congregation of Women prays for love, children, health and spiritual blessing often in loose rhyme. In doing so, these women battle the forces of darkness with the powers of light. They struggle to bloom like wildflowers by the banks of the Grand River where they often gather. Rooted in earth and stretching toward the brilliance of sun and moon many blossom like fertile wombs.

April Bulmer

Cambridge, Ontario, Canada

Congregation of Women

Spiritual Poems
by Those Who Battle
the Darkness and the Dim

Andrea

She is woman
the curve of light
and heart
a red fruit.
Girdle of bone
a sash like a serpent.
Her cassock, its cowl.
Beneath she is nude.

She blesses the altar
a bowl of apples
and a jug of water.
We take from her hands:
Mother Scarlett
her fruit and its blood.

Lily

Women in their cotton shifts.
Mother Scarlett, her heart.
She opens full lips
to sing
consecrates a bowl of apples
their skins red.
It is autumn
our hearts ripe:
flesh and pips
the core within.
The fruits of summer rain
and light.

Anne

The river, her green skin.
We gather on the new moon:
prayer and hymn.

Mother Scarlett, her hair
long and red as serpents.

I hear the Goddess in worship.

I wade her waters and bathe.
My body washed clean
of its rash and salve.

I turn rough stone
in my hands.
Offer thanks
to water
its nave and its apse.

Iris

Mother Scarlett preaches
from the heart
for it is a blossom.
It strains towards light
and opens in the dim of night
like moonflower
or woman.

My sisters and I kneel
at the altar.
Sip from a cup
of cold water.

For Goddess flows
wide at the Grand.
Her hips and her river.
The shadows
of her daughters.
We dance in our skirts
and sing of rain:
her God, her lover.

Milly

We rest on the bank
of the river:
Mother Scarlett and her women.
One vision we share:
a choir of fish
a congregation of turtles.
Pearl lifts the hem of her frock.
Old Martha discards her girdle.

Avery

It is close with heat.
My sisters and I
dip our feet.
Our shoes
like turtles on the bank.

I pull myself through the river.
The hem of my skirt damp.
I rest then with the women
on the shore.

The rains come.
Soft mud.
Our footprints
and our prayers
washed into the current
like clippings
that new moon
we cut our hair.

Ashley

Daddy called her a breed
my new friend, Wanda Bearskin.
He said she smelled like a coon.
We played with bones, small and fine:
a crow fallen on a blood moon.
A nest too, empty as Daddy's heart.
My own heart blue and fragile as an egg.
Wanda's a red bird.
"Listen," she said. "It beats like wings."
I pressed my cheek to her chest.
The steady rhythm.
My heart opened, gasped
and sang this new hymn:
"Praise be to Wanda Bearskin. Amen."

Hole in the Sky

My man has passed.
His ashes tossed
into a field
of blue flax.

Women have left tobacco.
Horses bow their heads.
I have made a prayer
and buried it in the uterus
of the earth.

My mind wild bird
in a cage of bone
for my man was a voice
in the wilderness.

I mourn for my man.
I dream of him.
His heart a kill
his chest a skin.
His ghost exhausted
and wounded.

But his light
a drum
a bloom
a morning moon.

Woman Who Blooms

My people drag hands
like paddles
through water.
On the shore
spirits shift like shadows.
Reeds bend as in prayer
with dim light.
Offer themselves
to the rhythm of rattles.

One Who Lives Below

St. Lucy, witch doctor
blesses my eyes:
a pale salve, her hands.
They heal darkness.
I bleed light.

I make a small shrine:
birch and tobacco
feather of magpie.

I see shadows
in the longhouse:
St. Lucy quivers.

When I come beneath Bobby Goodnets
his face is tough.

All night, Lucy applies
an ointment.
It is thick and cool.

Lucy, saint of the blind
and healer of Bobby:
once angel turnip, hard gourd.

Isabella

St. Lucy, my daughter wears
your crown of light:
candles balanced
on a wreath.

Outside, even dead leaves
open their palms.
The Congregation of Women breathes.
Prayers flicker in our hearts:
tallow and wick.

We fall to our knees.
My daughter
her hat of wax
bleeds.

Brooke

My soul rose:
new stem from old root.
My eyes opened
to light.

This morning
the sun too
is born again.
His many lives:
their radiant blood
and skin.

Maris

Menses coils in my pelvis.

How weary I am
as I shed my blood.
The red skin of serpent.

Dawn

Released from the cage
of my hips
like a frail bird
I break and bleed.

For the Goddess
and her moon
wax the lining
of my womb.

My tablets and rags
shallow bowls and cloth.
I wash blood and roots
the ghosts of ancestors:
damp and loose.

I rehearse the menses creed.

The spirits of old–
the Irish and the Danes–
will die in me
like dreams.

Sophie

Come, lover, for I am damp tonight.
Then, the sun rises like you.
Light on my body.

I move in and out of dream:
a mirage.
You are a nomad dropping to your knees.
Your head rag loose.
You mop your brow with it
and the shadow on my skin.
I am swabbed by your gauze.
But I, too, am of cloth:
my hymen a torn ribbon
the fabric of virgins.

Tomorrow, my bloods:
the stained linen of women.

Beth

A murder of crows
like rags discarded near my truck.
The exhaust and my breath.
I think of God.

Red berries on a tree.
I am on my bloods.

A bucket on my flatbed:
the wind makes hard love.

Gillian

Once I loved a boy
his eyes the shade
of copper coins.
He would not dance
with me.
I held myself like a shawl
and wore soft pads
against my loins.
My heart burned for him
like a candle.
The wick sturdy and trimmed.
For I imagined his breath
and the soft cream
of my tallow.

Sue

Mother tells of the moon:
big now and bright
it waxes.
How cold it is.
The trees bow
in the wind.
My dog shivers.
My heart, too, on its axis.

Meg

It is morning
the geese cry
in the grey sky.
The sun a rag.

The dog and I breathe
on Albert St.
Winter ghosts
drag their gowns
in wet snow.

A procession, a hymn.
Their song rises on the wind.

The cold like a wafer
on the tongue:
a thin host.

Kathryn

She has left for the other world
without her wedding rings
and little gold watch.
Her hair is thin
and she is so pale
in the full moonlight.
Her husband washes
her body with a cloth.
Early spring
her tree a skeleton.
Jesus is in the tomb.
Women bring spices and ointment.

We will cremate her body
and store her ashes in an urn.
Bury them near the ancestors:
early kin.
Their bones shift like babes
in womb-skin.

Charlene

Taurus opens her fat thighs
and births a new life:
my father, 1929.

Even the moon down.
His mother's breast
a soggy bloom.

At 19, they lock him
in a little room.
He eats creamed peas
and sleeps.

He dreams of the sun
a candle:
wick and tallow.

But he is of shadows.
Those haunts and shades
who genuflect at graves.

Elle

We celebrate on the new moon:
pink cake and small flames
in the month of May.

I was drawn from your belly.
Born of a scar.
Birthmark under a thumb.

But the earth opened
her thighs
and heaved a little weight:
a shadow on the bed
stems and buds.
Roots new to faith.

Martha

Sunlight sinks
into the soft loins
of earth.

And I pray my man
might open
my petals
their moist pink blooms.

Betty

Women in light frocks.
We feed on apricots.
My issue of blood.

Rituals of love
bloom in summer:
morning moon
like a host.

Tongue of river.

Winifred

How quiet my heart
a still pond
in the dim.
Perhaps, a lotus blooms.
Its roots grounded
in the soft earth.
It opens to morning
balanced on its stem.

The delicate petals
flower and fall.
Then bud again.

Yes, I am of the Goddess:
her seasons
her cycles
her rhythm. Amen.

Honey

A blood moon:
a basin
a ceramic bowl
or the hips
of the Goddess
and her gauze
her ache.

I am a woman:
the wax and wane
of my womb.
Today, I am a crescent
and my breasts
a small weight.

Touch me husband
and I will swell.
Her majesty and I
bearing the fullness
of light.
Pregnant, dragging waters
and seeds in soil.
Fertile and great.

Beryl

The moon is full
and I am great-with-blood.
Womb sheds her lining
like wine from a cup.
The Goddess moves in me
like breeze in a curtain.
She made cloth
and soft napkins
tampons–once rolls of Egyptian papyrus–
for women.

But Jesus did not raise his goblet
to the curve of waist or bust.
Mothers prepare your daughters
with offerings of milk to the Goddess.
Hang garlands from the girdle.
Bloom roses:
stained layers of gauze.

April

Watercolours.
Mama stirs her paintbrush.
Her flower a teacup.
Steep of sunlight
and warm rain.

Perhaps, the Goddess
sipped from the lip.
A soft imprint
of her mouth.
Scent of divine breath
on the bloom.

Eternal Blossom

Mother Scarlett
kneels
among a sacrifice
of flowers
and lifts a bloom:
a chalice
to her lips.

Ruth

My breasts,
heavy with light
and the weight of rain.
Their tender red buds.

The Congregation of Women
our gowns of linen.
We anoint our flesh
with jars of salve
ointment and rub.

The fragrant scent of balm
as we perspire
beneath the sun.

Clementine

God's soft body
against mine.
His breath an old woman's.
I worship His lungs
the gentle rise and fall
and the consumptive cough.

His hand
on my breast
eclipses a moon:
a swell of cloth.

Mother Scarlett

An angel fallen.
We wrap her
sweet and dusty in linen.

Her breasts full moons.

A ceremony
a simple grace.
The shadows of women
their wide hips
their loose black lace.

Heaving and crying
at the hole.
The rains come.
A wet rag.
My damp soul.

I whimper
like a shivering dog.

Even the river is blue.

Margaret

Mother Scarlett, the phases of her heart.
And my sisters, their shadows
kneel like the river
before light and stone.

Mother, her eyes
like minnows
swim over our poems.

Doctor Rowen

Mother Scarlett, her breasts
soft as gloves.
Girdle of bone
and belly great-with-love.

The child, a weight
she carries low
beneath her cassock.
I imagine its heart
a bloom.

In the fullness of time:
Mother Scarlett
blood in the dirt.

We will anoint
her girl
with river and moon.

Marla

Mother Scarlett and her man
love in the dark.
A babe, a heart.
Its hinge
and the crushed velvet
of an antique locket.

Opal

My heart its rusty lock.
You bear the skeleton key.
It opens.
The face of our child tattooed there.
Her eyes dark moons. Her mouth a scar.
Her heart, perhaps, light, then flower.
Brief then broken in an early hour.

Grace

I wear my mother's watch
though the hands are slow.
But time is only my heartbeat:
the clumsy genuflect
at the high altar
of blood.

Jane

Husband calls me sweetheart
and strokes my permanent wave.
I am great with his child.
A boy hiding behind drapery.
I dream his dreams.
It is winter.
Halleluiah steady as breath
in the cold rain.

Chris

The scent of oranges at winter solstice.
Johnny's heart in its tough skin.
All night
his seed, his fruit.

In the morning,
a winter moon
fades in the cold.

The liturgy of the body.
Johnny and I balanced
on our knees
sighing *Amen*.
Sweet juice on our tongues.

Sugar

We gather by the river.
There is a wind.
The Holy Spirit shivers.
I pray for C.
He dwells in the next county.
I imagine his truck:
it moves through snow
like a tired bison.

The Congregation of Women.
Our hymn, a leaf.
How it turns in the cold:
I sing for C.

We fall to our knees.
A flock of damp wool.
We gather our shawls:
we are women of the caul.

Celeste

My husband weeps
against my bosom.
How tender the breasts.

Today, the wind.
It whines like a dog.
Our son a spirit now.
I imagine his soft gloves
massage the wide hips
of the river.
Perhaps, he kneels there.
It is winter.
He only dreams of crow.

My husband, his heart—
a December moon—
sets low.

Fern

An adagio of nature
as it stretches its limbs
after the chill of winter.
Develops the flexible muscle
and dance of spring.

Dotty

Lilies are bells
and will ring
with the light of Christ.
Bloom their hymns of white.

Charlotte

You are spirit.
Your hands are spring leaves.
You touch my breasts
for they are skins
heavy with the weight
of milk.
Our babe breathes.

You passed before
I pushed and pushed
and gave forth.

I anoint her with
soaps and lotions.

Her body is pale
the shade of orchid
and her mouth too
is a flower
red and open.

Whitney

It rains today.
I am so slow.
My body is swollen
and my womb
haunts me
with the spirit of woman
and your ghost.

For you are not a man
but a warlock.
All night your spells.

I dreamt of a snake
and the sleeve of its skin.
There was a moon
and her hips blossomed.

Mag

My broom
its hair tangled
with dust.
I brush it with a rag.

My spells are clots
of milk
clabbered in a bucket.
I stir the curds
soft and white
as cloth.

Violet

My new boots
soft prints
on the earth:
an autograph.
My signature:
shapes in the dirt.
A scar, a truth.

The weight of my soul
like the river.
Its force and its stones.
I bear this and the burden
of my body too
as I lift each foot
and stroll.

Greer

A tortoise on the bank
of the river.
Mother Scarlett
lays hands
on her shell.
The Great Potter's bowl.
I bless and anoint it
with oil.

Millicent

I am great-with-child.
The women bless my mound.
Laying on of hands.
They anoint my belly
with dewberry.
The sweet scent.

I am a tel
beneath the sun.
Baby an artifact
a relic from a life
of fire and blood.

She will come again.
We will bathe her
in the water
wash the visions
from her eyes
with soft rags and rub
and the river of daughters.
St. Lucy too
will apply a little mud.
Soon, they will flower.

Hannah

Jesus hair loose and long
when he took Da.
It was the day
we hauled water.
A bucket in my husband's hand.
A damp sleeve.

Sister L—set the body:
a rag, a cake of goats milk.

But my heart:
its faded colours
and wilt.

Harriet

I only dream
of morning—
the sun a blossom—
for my eyes are damp
and dark as seeds.

The memory of
the moon.
My daughter's face
pale as trillium
for she flowered
in my womb.

Come, St. Lucy.
I am blind.
Bless me
that my eyes
open like buds
bloom beneath
your light.

Dusty

We wed
on the summer solstice.
The sun birthed light
in the night
and so did you and I.

Our shadows, too, walked
the labyrinth.
We were one in the centre
for Mother Scarlett
blessed our roots and
blossoming sighs.

Husband, I love you
on the longest day
and in the dim of winter.
My heart
a bed of seeds
blooms in your beams.
I will bear you
the fruits of autumn:
the ripening flesh
of sons and daughters.

Samantha

Eve, you were born
of his rib
a parenthesis.

He peeled your heart
like the apple.
How vulnerable the flesh
and pips.
So, you wrote him a poem
in the dirt:
the sensitivity of fruit.
"Beneath the skin
a core, a creed."

Blanche

I wait for Jesus
in my garden
among petunias
and strawberry plants.

Gabrielle washes windows.
I rehearse a liturgical dance.

The full moon is in Sagittarius.

I wear a dress of gauze
sandals on my feet.
I will tell Jesus of my dreams:
mothers, their calcified teats.

I wait for Jesus
throw my arms to the light.
I turn like a wind chime.

All evening I listen
to the tongues of toads
and night birds
who sing of eggs
and the dream
of new mouths.

I am a barren woman
who prays Jesus:
I open my body
like the door
of a rusty cage.
My spirit flies
nests in the lap
of apple tree.

Rose

I wish to anoint
my women
and minister to their souls
but my tongue
rises and falls
in my mouth
like the clapper
of a bell.
I think of Moses.

I wrote a song
but stammer.
My hands tremble
and St. Luke's oil
spills.
It is a pale puddle
on the earth.
Perhaps, though
it will heal her there
in the soft spot
where Goddess
pushed and pushed,
and gave birth.

Lisa

My man's hair long as Jesus'.
The shade of crow.
And his body
an attitude of worship
like a bird.
His soft head palsied.

He enters my body:
a hollow
like the hole in a tree.
A place for something wild
to nest.
Though I am naked and quiet:
the damp and the bones.

Together, our breath a silent creed.

Faith

We pitch a tent
of skins
and beneath I open
to your love.

Then I dream
we shuffle
to the rhythm
of an old religion.
I am a vase of blood.

In the morning
dim memories.
But light stretches
from my small space.
Perhaps, I will bloom:
a damp flower
her roots torn.
Hair like bishop's lace.

Ruby

In an early time
Goddess bore the sun.
His hair the shade
of late autumn.

Her nipples swelled
with the heat
of son's mouth.

She also birthed
the moon
and restored the sky
to health.
For she stitched the tear
when sky opened her thighs.
A rent curtain
for the birth of Christ.

Peg

Christ's heart
a fragile egg
blue in its shell.

It hatched, a small bird.
It sang a little song.

A feathered mass.
It beat from his chest:
an empty womb.

Meredith

We bury my dog
in a womb of earth.
Her spirit will rest
in the lap
of the Lord:
soft pats, perhaps:
a little woof.

Still, my heart is a grave.

I imagine it a bouquet:
flowers that open
and beautifully bleed.

Margie

Lover cradles me
in the boughs of his arms.
My heart is a bud
then a leaf:
its veins and its blood.

We are old souls:
the rings of time
the design of a god
and the freedom
of seed and shadow
light and sun.

Lover and I
in an earlier life.
Our dirty feet
rooted in earth.
Our spines
and their sap.
We reached like spires.
How we weathered the days:
baptism of rain.
Though we bowed then
in a gentle wind
beneath the moon:
altar of night.

Clara

Your mother has passed.
She sleeps now beneath
the moons of Saturn.
Her breath ragged
and her face a torn bloom.
Death has lined her palms
etched like runes.

We gather in the chapel
and fall to our knees.
Flowers die slowly
as we sing
and silently breathe.

Soon, she will visit you
perhaps in the dim.
Balanced on canes
bloody gauze on her chin.
Hold her then
for soon she will rise.
Heal with the Goddess
God's nurse of the skies.

June

The sun a golden coin
as it was in Rome
when the Goddess
her hair
its sweet-smelling perfume.
Her garment of flax
hobnail shoes.
She dusted her eyelids
with saffron
with ochre she rouged.

We offer her honey cakes
figs and plums.
The seeds of pomegranate
and nightingale tongues.
Olives and dates
even the memory of slaves
and fish sauce we stir
in jars of clay.

Babette

Lord, You come as spirit
pass light
through my lungs.
I exhale You
Your risen breath.

All night I dream of love.
It is a seed
the heart blooms.
Its petals blood red
and tender as tea rose.

Briefly briefly it grows
beneath Your beams
as You brighten the dim
of the enemy's shadow.

Elizabeth

In the cave of my chest
is a slow heart:
a turtle
her soft belly.
Etched like a palm:
lifeline, mount of Venus.

Her hard green shell.
She pokes like a thumb
from a fist of flesh.

Your heart
a conch.
I listen
to the rhythm of the sea.
Its foam, perhaps
a signature of light.
A script: your name
and your deity.

Bronwen

Daughter, I will not overshadow your precious light
and dim its bright blooms.
Write your spiritual psalms
and offer them to the goddess of night long:
healing balms of sunshine for her
and those stumbling in the dark
their hearts flickering with short wicks.
Spirit is calling you to this
and me something else only dreams foretell.
Perhaps, I will be well or feverishly sick.

Grammy

I dream my heart is a blue thing
a little purse:
keys and coins and a cotton handkerchief
damp with curse.
The skin of the bag and its scars.

But my mother's rub:
a pale salve and a chamois.
My heart supple then to the touch.
Clean and stuffed with love.

All night the moon too
a sack heavy with rouge and balm
and a note from her mom...

Something falls from the sky:
leather glove?

But in the morning
I imagine the sun
a mirror.
Goddess, her bright reflection:
her soft, pierced ears.

Acknowledgments

"June" placed in the Food For Thought Contest, "Beth" in the Ultra Short Poem Competition and an early version of "Sugar" in the Arborealis Competition Chapbook all run by The Ontario Poetry Society. "Greer" appeared in "Verse Afire, May to August, 2017." "Anna" and "Clara" were winners in the Cambridge Poem-A-Day Contest (2015 and 2016). "Fern" and "Brooke" were published in TVOntario Prime-Timers newsletters. "Isabella" appeared in *The Cambridge Citizen* and a version of "Hole in the Sky" in *Prairie Clan* on the Internet. A version of "Bronwen" was published in *Piping at the End of Days: A Book of Overcoming.*

Bio Note:

April Bulmer has had several other books published. She holds Master's degrees in creative writing, religious studies (women and religion) and theological studies. She lives in Cambridge, Ontario but was born and raised in Toronto where she worked at TVOntario and *Maclean's* magazine. Her work has been set to women's choir music at the Oberlin Conservatory in Ohio and has been published widely in prestigious journals, magazines and newspapers. April has received many grants and awards for her work which often addresses the role and magic of the divine feminine.

Contact her at april.poet@bell.net.

List of Previously Published Titles

Creeds and Remedies: The Feminine and Religion in Waterloo Region (Serengeti Press), 2017

And With Thy Spirit (Hidden Brook Press), 2016

Women of the Cloth (Black Moss Press), 2013

The Goddess Psalms (Serengeti Press), 2008

Black Blooms (Serengeti Press), 2007

Holy Land (Serengeti Press), 2006

Mustard Seeds (Leaf Press), 2005

Spring Rain (Serengeti Press), 2004

Oh My Goddess (Serengeti Press), 2004

HIM (Black Moss Press), 1999

The Weight of Wings (Trout Lily Press), 1997

A Salve For Every Sore (Cormorant Books), 1991